50 Classic Comforts: Hearty meals for Every Season

By: Kelly Johnson

Table of Contents

- Beef Stew
- Chicken Pot Pie
- Meatloaf
- Macaroni and Cheese
- Baked Ziti
- Shepherd's Pie
- Pot Roast
- Clam Chowder
- Lasagna
- Baked Chicken Alfredo
- Sloppy Joes
- Chili
- Chicken and Rice Casserole
- Chicken Fried Rice
- Sweet and Sour Pork
- Beef Tacos
- Spaghetti Bolognese

- French Onion Soup
- Eggplant Parmesan
- Roast Chicken
- Fish and Chips
- Beef and Broccoli Stir Fry
- Chicken and Vegetable Stir Fry
- Chicken Parmesan
- Stuffed Bell Peppers
- Beef and Vegetable Soup
- Sliders
- Buffalo Wings
- Cornbread and Chili
- Grilled Cheese and Tomato Soup
- Chicken Noodle Soup
- Sausage and Peppers
- Grilled Steak with Roasted Vegetables
- BBQ Ribs
- Pulled Pork Sandwiches
- Roasted Salmon

- Pork Schnitzel
- Potatoes au Gratin
- Risotto
- Chicken Caesar Salad
- Sausage and Mushroom Risotto
- Vegetable Frittata
- Beef Empanadas
- Cornish Hen with Stuffing
- Beef Wellington
- Fried Chicken and Mashed Potatoes
- Ratatouille
- Beef Chili with Cornbread
- Shrimp Scampi
- Grilled Pork Chops

Beef Stew

Ingredients:

- 2 lbs beef stew meat, cubed
- 4 cups beef broth
- 2 cups carrots, sliced
- 2 cups potatoes, diced
- 1 onion, chopped
- 2 cloves garlic, minced
- 1 cup frozen peas
- 1/2 cup flour
- 2 tbsp vegetable oil
- 1 tsp thyme
- 1 bay leaf
- Salt and pepper to taste

Instructions:

1. In a large pot, heat vegetable oil over medium-high heat. Brown the beef stew meat in batches, then set aside.
2. In the same pot, sauté onions and garlic until softened.
3. Sprinkle flour over the onions and garlic, stirring to form a roux.
4. Slowly add beef broth while stirring to avoid lumps.

5. Return the beef to the pot, add carrots, potatoes, thyme, bay leaf, salt, and pepper.

6. Bring to a boil, then reduce the heat and simmer for 1-2 hours until the beef is tender.

7. Stir in peas and cook for an additional 5 minutes.

8. Remove the bay leaf and serve.

Chicken Pot Pie

Ingredients:

- 2 cups cooked chicken, shredded
- 1 cup frozen peas and carrots
- 1/2 cup butter
- 1/3 cup flour
- 2 cups chicken broth
- 1 cup milk
- 1 tsp thyme
- 1/2 tsp salt
- 1/4 tsp black pepper
- 1 package refrigerated pie crusts (or homemade crust)

Instructions:

1. Preheat the oven to 425°F (220°C).
2. In a large saucepan, melt butter over medium heat. Stir in flour to form a roux.
3. Gradually whisk in chicken broth and milk. Continue stirring until the mixture thickens.
4. Add cooked chicken, peas, carrots, thyme, salt, and pepper. Stir to combine.
5. Unroll one pie crust and fit it into a pie dish. Pour the chicken mixture into the crust.

6. Place the second pie crust on top, crimping the edges to seal. Cut a few slits in the top crust for steam to escape.

7. Bake for 30-35 minutes, or until the crust is golden brown.

8. Let it cool for a few minutes before serving.

Meatloaf

Ingredients:

- 1 lb ground beef
- 1/2 lb ground pork
- 1 cup breadcrumbs
- 1/4 cup milk
- 1/4 cup ketchup
- 1 egg, beaten
- 1 onion, chopped
- 2 cloves garlic, minced
- 1 tsp salt
- 1/2 tsp black pepper
- 1/4 tsp dried thyme
- 1/4 cup ketchup (for topping)

Instructions:

1. Preheat the oven to 350°F (175°C).
2. In a large bowl, combine ground beef, ground pork, breadcrumbs, milk, ketchup, egg, onion, garlic, salt, pepper, and thyme.
3. Transfer the meat mixture to a loaf pan and shape it into a loaf.
4. Spread ketchup over the top of the meatloaf.

5. Bake for 1 hour, or until the meatloaf reaches an internal temperature of 160°F (71°C).

6. Let it rest for 10 minutes before slicing and serving.

Macaroni and Cheese

Ingredients:

- 8 oz elbow macaroni
- 2 cups shredded sharp cheddar cheese
- 1 cup milk
- 1/4 cup butter
- 2 tbsp flour
- 1/2 tsp salt
- 1/4 tsp black pepper
- 1/4 tsp paprika (optional)

Instructions:

1. Cook the macaroni according to the package directions, then drain and set aside.
2. In a saucepan, melt butter over medium heat. Stir in flour to form a roux.
3. Gradually add milk, whisking continuously until the sauce thickens.
4. Stir in shredded cheese, salt, pepper, and paprika until the cheese melts and the sauce is smooth.
5. Combine the cheese sauce with the cooked macaroni and stir to coat.
6. Serve immediately.

Baked Ziti

Ingredients:

- 1 lb ziti pasta
- 2 cups marinara sauce
- 1 1/2 cups ricotta cheese
- 2 cups shredded mozzarella cheese
- 1/4 cup grated Parmesan cheese
- 1 tsp dried basil
- 1/2 tsp dried oregano
- Salt and pepper to taste

Instructions:

1. Preheat the oven to 375°F (190°C).
2. Cook the ziti pasta according to the package directions, then drain and set aside.
3. In a large bowl, mix together marinara sauce, ricotta cheese, mozzarella, Parmesan, basil, oregano, salt, and pepper.
4. Combine the cooked pasta with the sauce mixture and stir to coat.
5. Transfer the pasta mixture to a greased baking dish and top with additional mozzarella cheese.
6. Bake for 25-30 minutes, or until the cheese is bubbly and golden.
7. Let it cool for a few minutes before serving.

Shepherd's Pie

Ingredients:

- 1 lb ground beef or lamb
- 1 onion, chopped
- 2 cloves garlic, minced
- 2 cups mixed vegetables (peas, carrots, corn)
- 1 cup beef broth
- 1 tbsp Worcestershire sauce
- 4 cups mashed potatoes
- 1/2 tsp salt
- 1/4 tsp black pepper

Instructions:

1. Preheat the oven to 400°F (200°C).
2. In a large skillet, cook ground beef or lamb over medium heat until browned.
3. Add onions and garlic, cooking until softened.
4. Stir in mixed vegetables, beef broth, and Worcestershire sauce. Simmer for 10 minutes.
5. Spread the meat mixture in a greased baking dish.
6. Spoon mashed potatoes over the meat mixture and spread evenly.
7. Bake for 20 minutes, or until the top is golden.

8. Serve hot.

Pot Roast

Ingredients:

- 3-4 lb chuck roast
- 4 cups beef broth
- 4 carrots, chopped
- 4 potatoes, chopped
- 1 onion, chopped
- 2 cloves garlic, minced
- 2 tbsp vegetable oil
- 1 tsp dried thyme
- 1 bay leaf
- Salt and pepper to taste

Instructions:

1. Preheat the oven to 350°F (175°C).
2. In a large ovenproof pot, heat vegetable oil over medium-high heat. Brown the roast on all sides, then remove and set aside.
3. In the same pot, sauté onions and garlic until softened.
4. Add beef broth, carrots, potatoes, thyme, bay leaf, salt, and pepper. Return the roast to the pot.
5. Cover and bake for 3-4 hours, or until the roast is fork-tender.

6. Slice the roast and serve with the vegetables.

Clam Chowder

Ingredients:

- 2 cups clams, chopped (or use canned clams)
- 1 cup clam juice
- 2 cups potatoes, diced
- 1 onion, chopped
- 2 cloves garlic, minced
- 1/4 cup butter
- 1 cup heavy cream
- 1 cup milk
- 1/2 tsp thyme
- Salt and pepper to taste

Instructions:

1. In a large pot, melt butter over medium heat. Sauté onions and garlic until softened.

2. Add diced potatoes and clam juice. Bring to a boil, then simmer for 10-15 minutes until potatoes are tender.

3. Stir in clams, heavy cream, milk, thyme, salt, and pepper.

4. Simmer for an additional 5 minutes.

5. Serve hot, garnished with fresh parsley if desired.

Lasagna

Ingredients:

- 9 lasagna noodles, cooked
- 2 cups ricotta cheese
- 2 cups mozzarella cheese, shredded
- 1/2 cup Parmesan cheese, grated
- 1 lb ground beef
- 2 cups marinara sauce
- 1 onion, chopped
- 2 cloves garlic, minced
- 1 egg, beaten
- 1 tsp dried basil
- Salt and pepper to taste

Instructions:

1. Preheat the oven to 375°F (190°C).
2. In a large skillet, cook ground beef, onions, and garlic until browned. Drain excess fat.
3. Add marinara sauce, basil, salt, and pepper to the beef mixture. Simmer for 10 minutes.
4. In a bowl, combine ricotta cheese, egg, and half of the Parmesan cheese.

5. In a baking dish, layer lasagna noodles, beef sauce, ricotta mixture, and mozzarella cheese. Repeat until all ingredients are used.

6. Top with remaining mozzarella and Parmesan.

7. Bake for 45 minutes, or until the cheese is bubbly and golden.

8. Let it rest for 10 minutes before serving.

Baked Chicken Alfredo

Ingredients:

- 2 cups cooked chicken, shredded
- 1 lb fettuccine pasta, cooked
- 2 cups Alfredo sauce
- 1/2 cup grated Parmesan cheese
- 1 cup mozzarella cheese, shredded
- 1 tbsp parsley, chopped (for garnish)

Instructions:

1. Preheat the oven to 350°F (175°C).
2. In a large bowl, combine cooked chicken, cooked fettuccine, Alfredo sauce, and half of the Parmesan cheese.
3. Transfer to a greased baking dish and top with mozzarella cheese and remaining Parmesan.
4. Bake for 20-25 minutes, or until the cheese is bubbly and golden.
5. Garnish with parsley and serve.

Sloppy Joes

Ingredients:

- 1 lb ground beef
- 1 onion, chopped
- 1 bell pepper, chopped
- 1 cup ketchup
- 1 tbsp Worcestershire sauce
- 1 tbsp brown sugar
- 1 tsp mustard
- 1 tsp garlic powder
- Salt and pepper to taste
- Hamburger buns

Instructions:

1. In a skillet, cook ground beef, onion, and bell pepper over medium heat until browned. Drain excess fat.
2. Stir in ketchup, Worcestershire sauce, brown sugar, mustard, garlic powder, salt, and pepper.
3. Simmer for 10 minutes, stirring occasionally.
4. Serve the sloppy joe mixture on hamburger buns.

Chili

Ingredients:

- 1 lb ground beef or turkey
- 1 onion, chopped
- 2 cloves garlic, minced
- 1 bell pepper, chopped
- 1 can (14.5 oz) diced tomatoes
- 1 can (15 oz) kidney beans, drained and rinsed
- 1 can (15 oz) black beans, drained and rinsed
- 1 can (6 oz) tomato paste
- 2 tbsp chili powder
- 1 tsp cumin
- 1 tsp paprika
- 1/2 tsp oregano
- Salt and pepper to taste
- 1 cup beef or chicken broth
- Optional toppings: sour cream, shredded cheese, chopped green onions

Instructions:

1. In a large pot, brown the ground meat over medium heat. Drain excess fat.

2. Add onion, garlic, and bell pepper to the pot and sauté until softened.

3. Stir in chili powder, cumin, paprika, oregano, salt, and pepper.

4. Add diced tomatoes, beans, tomato paste, and broth. Stir to combine.

5. Bring to a boil, then reduce heat and simmer for 30-45 minutes, stirring occasionally.

6. Serve with optional toppings.

Chicken and Rice Casserole

Ingredients:

- 2 cups cooked chicken, shredded
- 1 1/2 cups white rice, cooked
- 1 can (10.5 oz) cream of chicken soup
- 1 cup chicken broth
- 1/2 cup shredded cheddar cheese
- 1/4 cup breadcrumbs
- 1 tsp garlic powder
- 1 tsp onion powder
- Salt and pepper to taste

Instructions:

1. Preheat the oven to 350°F (175°C).
2. In a large bowl, mix together the chicken, rice, cream of chicken soup, chicken broth, garlic powder, onion powder, salt, and pepper.
3. Transfer the mixture to a greased baking dish and top with shredded cheddar cheese.
4. Sprinkle breadcrumbs on top.
5. Bake for 25-30 minutes, or until the cheese is bubbly and the casserole is hot.
6. Serve and enjoy.

Chicken Fried Rice

Ingredients:

- 2 cups cooked rice (preferably cold)
- 2 tbsp vegetable oil
- 2 boneless, skinless chicken breasts, diced
- 1/2 onion, chopped
- 2 cloves garlic, minced
- 1/2 cup frozen peas and carrots
- 2 eggs, scrambled
- 3 tbsp soy sauce
- 1 tsp sesame oil
- 1/4 tsp black pepper

Instructions:

1. In a large skillet or wok, heat vegetable oil over medium-high heat. Add diced chicken and cook until browned and cooked through. Remove from the skillet and set aside.

2. In the same skillet, sauté onion and garlic until softened.

3. Add peas and carrots and cook for a few minutes.

4. Push the vegetables to one side and scramble the eggs in the empty space.

5. Add the cooked rice, chicken, soy sauce, sesame oil, and black pepper. Stir to combine and cook for 5-7 minutes, until everything is heated through.

6. Serve hot.

Sweet and Sour Pork

Ingredients:

- 1 lb pork tenderloin, cut into bite-sized cubes
- 1/2 cup cornstarch
- 1 egg, beaten
- 1/2 cup vegetable oil (for frying)
- 1/2 bell pepper, chopped
- 1/2 onion, chopped
- 1/2 cup pineapple chunks
- 1/4 cup rice vinegar
- 1/4 cup ketchup
- 1/4 cup sugar
- 2 tbsp soy sauce

Instructions:

1. Coat the pork cubes in cornstarch and dip them in the beaten egg.
2. In a large skillet or wok, heat vegetable oil over medium-high heat. Fry the pork in batches until golden brown, then remove and set aside.
3. In the same skillet, sauté bell pepper, onion, and pineapple until softened.
4. In a small bowl, whisk together rice vinegar, ketchup, sugar, and soy sauce.
5. Add the sauce to the skillet and stir to combine. Bring to a simmer.

6. Return the fried pork to the skillet and toss to coat in the sauce. Cook for an additional 5 minutes, until heated through.

7. Serve hot with steamed rice.

Beef Tacos

Ingredients:

- 1 lb ground beef
- 1 packet taco seasoning
- 1/4 cup water
- 8 small taco shells
- Toppings: shredded lettuce, chopped tomatoes, shredded cheese, sour cream, salsa

Instructions:

1. In a skillet, cook the ground beef over medium heat until browned. Drain excess fat.
2. Stir in taco seasoning and water. Simmer for 5-7 minutes.
3. Warm the taco shells according to package directions.
4. Fill each taco shell with the beef mixture and top with your favorite toppings.
5. Serve and enjoy!

Spaghetti Bolognese

Ingredients:

- 1 lb ground beef or pork
- 1 onion, chopped
- 2 cloves garlic, minced
- 1 can (14.5 oz) diced tomatoes
- 1/4 cup tomato paste
- 1/4 cup red wine (optional)
- 1 tsp dried basil
- 1/2 tsp dried oregano
- Salt and pepper to taste
- 1 lb spaghetti pasta
- Parmesan cheese, grated (optional)

Instructions:

1. In a large skillet, cook ground meat with onion and garlic until browned. Drain excess fat.
2. Stir in diced tomatoes, tomato paste, red wine (if using), basil, oregano, salt, and pepper. Simmer for 30 minutes, stirring occasionally.
3. While the sauce is simmering, cook the spaghetti according to package directions. Drain.

4. Serve the Bolognese sauce over the spaghetti and top with grated Parmesan cheese, if desired.

French Onion Soup

Ingredients:

- 4 large onions, thinly sliced
- 2 tbsp butter
- 1 tbsp olive oil
- 2 cloves garlic, minced
- 1/4 cup dry white wine (optional)
- 4 cups beef broth
- 1 tsp dried thyme
- 1 bay leaf
- 8 slices baguette
- 2 cups shredded Gruyère cheese

Instructions:

1. In a large pot, melt butter and olive oil over medium heat. Add onions and cook, stirring occasionally, until softened and caramelized (about 30-40 minutes).
2. Add garlic and cook for 1-2 minutes.
3. Pour in white wine (if using), scraping up any browned bits from the bottom of the pot.
4. Add beef broth, thyme, and bay leaf. Bring to a simmer and cook for 20 minutes.
5. Preheat the broiler.

6. Ladle soup into oven-safe bowls, top with a slice of baguette, and sprinkle with Gruyère cheese.

7. Place the bowls under the broiler for 2-3 minutes, or until the cheese is melted and bubbly.

8. Serve hot.

Eggplant Parmesan

Ingredients:

- 2 medium eggplants, sliced into 1/2-inch rounds
- 2 cups marinara sauce
- 2 cups mozzarella cheese, shredded
- 1/2 cup Parmesan cheese, grated
- 2 eggs, beaten
- 1 cup breadcrumbs
- 1/4 cup flour
- Salt and pepper to taste
- Olive oil for frying

Instructions:

1. Preheat the oven to 375°F (190°C).
2. Season eggplant slices with salt and let them sit for 20 minutes to draw out moisture. Pat dry with paper towels.
3. Dredge eggplant slices in flour, dip in beaten eggs, then coat with breadcrumbs.
4. Heat olive oil in a skillet over medium heat and fry eggplant slices until golden brown on both sides. Remove and set aside on paper towels.
5. In a baking dish, spread a thin layer of marinara sauce. Layer fried eggplant, sauce, mozzarella, and Parmesan. Repeat until all ingredients are used.
6. Top with mozzarella and Parmesan.

7. Bake for 25-30 minutes, or until the cheese is bubbly and golden.

8. Serve hot with pasta or a side salad.

Roast Chicken

Ingredients:

- 1 whole chicken (3-4 lbs)
- 2 tbsp olive oil
- 1 lemon, quartered
- 1 head garlic, halved
- 1 tsp rosemary
- 1 tsp thyme
- Salt and pepper to taste

Instructions:

1. Preheat the oven to 425°F (220°C).
2. Rub the chicken with olive oil and season with salt, pepper, rosemary, and thyme.
3. Stuff the chicken cavity with lemon quarters and garlic.
4. Roast for 1-1.5 hours, or until the internal temperature reaches 165°F (74°C).
5. Let the chicken rest for 10 minutes before carving and serving.

Fish and Chips

Ingredients:

- 4 white fish fillets (cod, haddock, or similar)
- 1 cup all-purpose flour
- 1 tsp baking powder
- 1/2 tsp salt
- 1/4 tsp black pepper
- 1 cup cold beer (or sparkling water)
- Vegetable oil for frying
- 4 large potatoes, cut into fries
- Salt to taste

Instructions:

1. Preheat oil in a deep fryer or large pot to 375°F (190°C).
2. For the fries, fry potato slices in batches for 3-5 minutes until golden. Remove and drain.
3. For the batter, whisk together flour, baking powder, salt, and pepper. Slowly add cold beer, whisking until smooth.
4. Dip fish fillets into the batter, then fry in hot oil for 4-5 minutes until golden and crispy.
5. Serve fish with fries, salt, and tartar sauce.

Beef and Broccoli Stir Fry

Ingredients:

- 1 lb flank steak or sirloin, thinly sliced
- 1 tbsp soy sauce
- 1 tbsp hoisin sauce
- 1 tbsp oyster sauce
- 2 tbsp vegetable oil
- 1 onion, sliced
- 3 cloves garlic, minced
- 1 tbsp fresh ginger, minced
- 2 cups broccoli florets
- 2 tbsp cornstarch mixed with 2 tbsp water (for thickening)
- Cooked rice for serving

Instructions:

1. In a small bowl, combine soy sauce, hoisin sauce, and oyster sauce. Set aside.
2. Heat vegetable oil in a large pan or wok over medium-high heat. Add the sliced beef and cook for 3-5 minutes, until browned. Remove from the pan and set aside.
3. In the same pan, add onion, garlic, and ginger. Sauté for 2-3 minutes until softened.
4. Add broccoli and stir-fry for 4-5 minutes until tender-crisp.

5. Return the beef to the pan and pour in the sauce mixture. Stir to coat. Add the cornstarch slurry and cook until the sauce thickens, about 1-2 minutes.

6. Serve over cooked rice.

Chicken and Vegetable Stir Fry

Ingredients:

- 2 boneless, skinless chicken breasts, thinly sliced
- 2 tbsp soy sauce
- 1 tbsp sesame oil
- 1 tbsp oyster sauce
- 1 tbsp honey
- 1 bell pepper, sliced
- 1 zucchini, sliced
- 1 cup snap peas
- 2 cloves garlic, minced
- 1 tbsp fresh ginger, minced
- Cooked rice for serving

Instructions:

1. In a small bowl, combine soy sauce, sesame oil, oyster sauce, and honey. Set aside.

2. Heat a large pan or wok over medium-high heat. Add the sliced chicken and cook for 5-7 minutes until browned and cooked through. Remove from the pan and set aside.

3. In the same pan, add garlic and ginger. Sauté for 1-2 minutes until fragrant.

4. Add bell pepper, zucchini, and snap peas. Stir-fry for 4-5 minutes until tender-crisp.

5. Return the chicken to the pan and pour in the sauce mixture. Stir to combine and cook for an additional 2-3 minutes.

6. Serve over cooked rice.

Chicken Parmesan

Ingredients:

- 4 boneless, skinless chicken breasts
- 1 cup breadcrumbs
- 1/2 cup grated Parmesan cheese
- 1 tsp garlic powder
- 1/2 tsp salt
- 1/4 tsp pepper
- 1 egg, beaten
- 1 cup marinara sauce
- 2 cups mozzarella cheese, shredded
- 2 tbsp olive oil
- Fresh basil for garnish (optional)

Instructions:

1. Preheat the oven to 375°F (190°C).
2. In a shallow bowl, mix breadcrumbs, Parmesan, garlic powder, salt, and pepper.
3. Dip each chicken breast into the beaten egg, then coat with the breadcrumb mixture.
4. Heat olive oil in a large skillet over medium heat. Cook the chicken breasts for 4-5 minutes on each side, until golden brown.

5. Transfer the chicken to a baking dish. Spoon marinara sauce over each piece, then top with mozzarella cheese.

6. Bake for 20 minutes, or until the chicken reaches 165°F (74°C).

7. Garnish with fresh basil, if desired. Serve with pasta or a side salad.

Stuffed Bell Peppers

Ingredients:

- 4 large bell peppers
- 1 lb ground beef or turkey
- 1 cup cooked rice
- 1 can (14.5 oz) diced tomatoes
- 1/2 onion, chopped
- 1 tsp garlic powder
- 1 tsp dried oregano
- 1/2 tsp salt
- 1/4 tsp black pepper
- 1/2 cup shredded cheddar cheese

Instructions:

1. Preheat the oven to 375°F (190°C).
2. Cut the tops off the bell peppers and remove the seeds.
3. In a skillet, cook the ground meat with onion until browned, breaking it apart as it cooks. Drain any excess fat.
4. Stir in cooked rice, diced tomatoes, garlic powder, oregano, salt, and pepper.
5. Stuff the peppers with the meat and rice mixture. Place them in a baking dish.
6. Top each stuffed pepper with shredded cheese.

7. Cover with foil and bake for 25-30 minutes. Remove the foil and bake for an additional 5-10 minutes to melt the cheese.

8. Serve hot.

Beef and Vegetable Soup

Ingredients:

- 1 lb stew beef, cubed
- 1 onion, chopped
- 2 carrots, sliced
- 2 potatoes, diced
- 2 celery stalks, chopped
- 3 cloves garlic, minced
- 1 can (14.5 oz) diced tomatoes
- 4 cups beef broth
- 1 bay leaf
- 1 tsp dried thyme
- Salt and pepper to taste

Instructions:

1. In a large pot, brown the stew beef over medium heat. Remove and set aside.
2. In the same pot, add onion, carrots, potatoes, and celery. Sauté for 5 minutes until vegetables begin to soften.
3. Add garlic and cook for 1 more minute.
4. Add diced tomatoes, beef broth, bay leaf, thyme, and browned beef. Bring to a boil.

5. Reduce heat and simmer for 45-60 minutes, or until the beef is tender.

6. Season with salt and pepper. Serve hot.

Sliders

Ingredients:

- 1 lb ground beef
- 1/2 tsp garlic powder
- 1/2 tsp onion powder
- Salt and pepper to taste
- 8 slider buns
- Cheese slices (optional)
- Lettuce, tomato, pickles for topping

Instructions:

1. Preheat the grill or a skillet over medium-high heat.
2. In a bowl, mix ground beef, garlic powder, onion powder, salt, and pepper.
3. Form the beef mixture into 8 small patties.
4. Grill or cook the patties for 3-4 minutes on each side, until fully cooked.
5. Toast the slider buns and assemble with the cooked patties and your desired toppings.
6. Serve hot.

Buffalo Wings

Ingredients:

- 10-12 chicken wings
- 1/4 cup butter, melted
- 1/2 cup hot sauce (such as Frank's RedHot)
- 1 tbsp white vinegar
- 1/2 tsp garlic powder
- 1/2 tsp onion powder
- Salt and pepper to taste
- Ranch or blue cheese dressing for dipping (optional)

Instructions:

1. Preheat the oven to 400°F (200°C).
2. Arrange the chicken wings on a baking sheet. Season with salt and pepper.
3. Bake for 25-30 minutes, flipping halfway, until crispy and fully cooked.
4. While the wings are baking, combine melted butter, hot sauce, vinegar, garlic powder, and onion powder in a bowl.
5. Toss the baked wings in the sauce mixture until evenly coated.
6. Serve with ranch or blue cheese dressing for dipping.

Cornbread and Chili

- **Cornbread:** See the previous recipe in our conversation for cornbread.

- **Chili:** See the previous recipe in our conversation for chili.

Serve them together for a classic comfort meal!

Grilled Cheese and Tomato Soup

Ingredients:

- 4 slices bread
- 4 slices cheddar cheese
- 2 tbsp butter
- 1 can (14.5 oz) tomato soup
- 1/4 cup cream (optional)
- Salt and pepper to taste

Instructions:

1. Butter one side of each slice of bread. Place one slice of cheese between two slices of bread.
2. Grill the sandwich in a skillet over medium heat until golden brown on both sides and the cheese is melted.
3. While the sandwich is cooking, heat the tomato soup in a pot over medium heat. Add cream, salt, and pepper if desired.
4. Serve the grilled cheese with the tomato soup for dipping.

Chicken Noodle Soup

Ingredients:

- 2 chicken breasts, cooked and shredded
- 4 cups chicken broth
- 2 carrots, sliced
- 2 celery stalks, chopped
- 1 onion, chopped
- 2 cloves garlic, minced
- 1 tsp dried thyme
- 1/2 tsp dried rosemary
- Salt and pepper to taste
- 2 cups egg noodles

Instructions:

1. In a large pot, sauté onion, carrots, celery, and garlic for 5 minutes until softened.
2. Add chicken broth, thyme, rosemary, and salt and pepper. Bring to a boil.
3. Add the shredded chicken and egg noodles. Reduce heat and simmer for 15-20 minutes, until the noodles are tender.
4. Serve hot.

Sausage and Peppers

Ingredients:

- 4 Italian sausages
- 2 bell peppers, sliced
- 1 onion, sliced
- 2 cloves garlic, minced
- 1/4 tsp red pepper flakes (optional)
- Salt and pepper to taste

Instructions:

1. Grill or cook the sausages in a skillet until browned and fully cooked.
2. In the same pan, sauté onion, bell peppers, and garlic until softened.
3. Slice the sausages and return them to the pan with the peppers and onions. Stir to combine.
4. Season with red pepper flakes, salt, and pepper.
5. Serve as is, or on a roll for a sandwich.

Grilled Steak with Roasted Vegetables

Ingredients:

- 2 ribeye or sirloin steaks
- 1 tbsp olive oil
- Salt and pepper to taste
- 1 lb mixed vegetables (carrots, potatoes, zucchini, etc.)
- 2 tbsp olive oil
- 1 tsp dried thyme
- 1 tsp dried rosemary

Instructions:

1. Preheat the grill to medium-high heat.
2. Rub steaks with olive oil and season with salt and pepper. Grill for 5-7 minutes on each side, depending on thickness and desired doneness.
3. Toss mixed vegetables with olive oil, thyme, rosemary, salt, and pepper. Roast in the oven at 400°F (200°C) for 25-30 minutes, stirring halfway, until tender.
4. Serve the steak with the roasted vegetables.

BBQ Ribs

Ingredients:

- 2 racks of baby back ribs
- 1/4 cup brown sugar
- 1/4 cup paprika
- 2 tbsp black pepper
- 1 tbsp salt
- 1 tbsp garlic powder
- 1 tbsp onion powder
- 1 tsp smoked paprika
- 1 tsp chili powder
- 1 tsp ground cumin
- 1 cup BBQ sauce (your choice)

Instructions:

1. Preheat the oven to 300°F (150°C).
2. Remove the membrane from the back of the ribs.
3. In a small bowl, combine brown sugar, paprika, black pepper, salt, garlic powder, onion powder, smoked paprika, chili powder, and cumin to make the dry rub.
4. Rub the spice mixture generously over the ribs.
5. Place the ribs on a baking sheet, cover with foil, and bake for 2.5-3 hours.

6. Preheat the grill to medium heat.

7. Brush the ribs with BBQ sauce and grill for an additional 10-15 minutes, turning occasionally.

8. Serve with extra BBQ sauce on the side.

Pulled Pork Sandwiches

Ingredients:

- 3-4 lbs pork shoulder
- 1 tbsp paprika
- 1 tbsp brown sugar
- 1 tbsp garlic powder
- 1 tbsp onion powder
- 1 tsp salt
- 1/2 tsp black pepper
- 1/2 tsp cumin
- 1/2 tsp chili powder
- 1 cup apple cider vinegar
- 1 cup BBQ sauce
- 8 hamburger buns

Instructions:

1. Preheat the oven to 300°F (150°C).
2. In a small bowl, combine paprika, brown sugar, garlic powder, onion powder, salt, pepper, cumin, and chili powder. Rub this mixture over the pork shoulder.
3. Place the pork shoulder in a large roasting pan and pour apple cider vinegar over the top.

4. Cover with foil and roast for 4-5 hours, or until the pork is tender and easily shreds.

5. Remove the pork from the oven and shred it using two forks.

6. Toss the shredded pork with BBQ sauce.

7. Serve on hamburger buns.

Roasted Salmon

Ingredients:

- 4 salmon fillets
- 2 tbsp olive oil
- 1 lemon, thinly sliced
- 2 cloves garlic, minced
- Salt and pepper to taste
- Fresh parsley, chopped (optional)

Instructions:

1. Preheat the oven to 400°F (200°C).
2. Place the salmon fillets on a baking sheet lined with parchment paper.
3. Drizzle olive oil over the fillets and sprinkle with garlic, salt, and pepper.
4. Place lemon slices on top of the salmon.
5. Roast for 12-15 minutes, or until the salmon flakes easily with a fork.
6. Garnish with fresh parsley, if desired.

Pork Schnitzel

Ingredients:

- 4 boneless pork chops
- 1 cup flour
- 2 eggs, beaten
- 2 cups breadcrumbs
- 1 tsp garlic powder
- 1 tsp paprika
- Salt and pepper to taste
- 2 tbsp vegetable oil
- Lemon wedges (for serving)

Instructions:

1. Pound the pork chops to an even thickness using a meat mallet.
2. Season the pork chops with salt, pepper, garlic powder, and paprika.
3. Dredge each pork chop in flour, dip into beaten eggs, and coat with breadcrumbs.
4. Heat vegetable oil in a large skillet over medium heat.
5. Fry the pork schnitzels for 3-4 minutes on each side, until golden brown and cooked through.
6. Serve with lemon wedges.

Potatoes au Gratin

Ingredients:

- 4 large potatoes, peeled and sliced thinly
- 2 cups heavy cream
- 2 cups shredded cheddar cheese
- 1/2 cup grated Parmesan cheese
- 1 clove garlic, minced
- 1 tbsp butter
- Salt and pepper to taste

Instructions:

1. Preheat the oven to 375°F (190°C).
2. Grease a 9x13-inch baking dish with butter.
3. Layer the sliced potatoes in the dish, overlapping slightly.
4. In a saucepan, heat the heavy cream, garlic, salt, and pepper over medium heat.
5. Pour the cream mixture over the potatoes.
6. Sprinkle shredded cheddar and Parmesan cheese on top.
7. Cover with foil and bake for 45 minutes.
8. Remove the foil and bake for an additional 15 minutes, until the top is golden brown and bubbly.

Risotto

Ingredients:

- 1 cup Arborio rice
- 1 small onion, finely chopped
- 2 cloves garlic, minced
- 4 cups chicken or vegetable broth, kept warm
- 1/2 cup dry white wine
- 2 tbsp butter
- 1/2 cup grated Parmesan cheese
- Salt and pepper to taste

Instructions:

1. In a large saucepan, melt 1 tablespoon of butter over medium heat.
2. Add onion and garlic and cook for 2-3 minutes, until softened.
3. Add the Arborio rice and stir for 1-2 minutes, until lightly toasted.
4. Add the white wine and stir until absorbed.
5. Gradually add the warm broth, 1/2 cup at a time, stirring constantly. Wait until the liquid is absorbed before adding more. Continue until the rice is creamy and cooked through, about 20-25 minutes.
6. Stir in the remaining butter and Parmesan cheese.
7. Season with salt and pepper to taste.

Chicken Caesar Salad

Ingredients:

- 2 boneless, skinless chicken breasts
- 6 cups Romaine lettuce, chopped
- 1/2 cup Caesar dressing
- 1/4 cup grated Parmesan cheese
- Croutons (optional)
- Salt and pepper to taste

Instructions:

1. Season the chicken breasts with salt and pepper. Grill or cook in a skillet over medium heat until fully cooked, about 6-7 minutes per side.
2. Slice the chicken into thin strips.
3. In a large bowl, toss the chopped Romaine lettuce with Caesar dressing.
4. Top with sliced chicken, grated Parmesan, and croutons, if desired.
5. Serve immediately.

Sausage and Mushroom Risotto

Ingredients:

- 1 cup Arborio rice
- 1/2 lb sausage (Italian or your choice), crumbled
- 1/2 lb mushrooms, sliced
- 1 small onion, chopped
- 2 cloves garlic, minced
- 4 cups chicken or vegetable broth, kept warm
- 1/2 cup dry white wine
- 2 tbsp butter
- 1/2 cup grated Parmesan cheese
- Salt and pepper to taste

Instructions:

1. In a large saucepan, cook sausage over medium heat until browned. Remove from the pan and set aside.
2. In the same pan, add mushrooms, onion, and garlic. Cook until softened, about 5 minutes.
3. Stir in the Arborio rice and cook for 1-2 minutes.
4. Add the white wine and stir until absorbed.
5. Gradually add warm broth, 1/2 cup at a time, stirring constantly, until the rice is creamy and cooked through, about 20-25 minutes.

6. Stir in sausage, butter, and Parmesan cheese.

7. Season with salt and pepper.

Vegetable Frittata

Ingredients:

- 8 eggs
- 1/2 cup milk
- 1 cup spinach, chopped
- 1/2 bell pepper, chopped
- 1/2 onion, chopped
- 1/2 cup cheese (cheddar, mozzarella, or your choice)
- Salt and pepper to taste
- Olive oil for greasing

Instructions:

1. Preheat the oven to 375°F (190°C).
2. In a bowl, whisk together eggs, milk, salt, and pepper.
3. Heat olive oil in a skillet over medium heat. Add bell pepper, onion, and spinach. Sauté for 3-4 minutes until softened.
4. Pour the egg mixture over the vegetables. Stir to combine, then sprinkle cheese on top.
5. Transfer the skillet to the oven and bake for 20-25 minutes, or until the frittata is set and golden brown.
6. Slice and serve warm.

Beef Empanadas

Ingredients:

- 1 lb ground beef
- 1/2 onion, chopped
- 1/2 cup olives, chopped
- 1/2 tsp cumin
- 1/2 tsp paprika
- 1/4 tsp chili powder
- 1/4 cup raisins (optional)
- 1 egg, beaten (for egg wash)
- 12 empanada dough circles (store-bought or homemade)

Instructions:

1. In a skillet, cook the ground beef and onion over medium heat until browned. Drain excess fat.
2. Add olives, cumin, paprika, chili powder, and raisins (if using). Stir to combine and cook for 3-4 minutes.
3. Preheat the oven to 375°F (190°C).
4. Place a spoonful of the beef mixture in the center of each empanada dough circle. Fold and press the edges to seal.
5. Brush each empanada with beaten egg.
6. Bake for 20-25 minutes, until golden brown.

Cornish Hen with Stuffing

Ingredients:

- 2 Cornish hens
- 1 cup stuffing mix
- 1/2 cup chicken broth
- 1/4 cup butter, melted
- Salt and pepper to taste
- Fresh herbs (rosemary, thyme) for garnish

Instructions:

1. Preheat the oven to 375°F (190°C).
2. Prepare the stuffing according to package instructions, using chicken broth and melted butter.
3. Stuff the Cornish hens with the prepared stuffing.
4. Season the hens with salt and pepper.
5. Roast the hens for 1 hour, or until the internal temperature reaches 165°F (75°C).
6. Garnish with fresh herbs before serving.

Beef Wellington

Ingredients:

- 2 lb beef tenderloin (center-cut)
- 2 tbsp olive oil
- 1/2 cup Dijon mustard
- 8 oz cremini or button mushrooms, finely chopped
- 1/4 cup shallots, finely chopped
- 2 cloves garlic, minced
- 1/4 cup dry white wine
- 8 oz prosciutto
- 1 sheet puff pastry
- 1 egg, beaten (for egg wash)
- Salt and pepper to taste

Instructions:

1. Preheat the oven to 400°F (200°C).

2. Season the beef tenderloin with salt and pepper. Heat olive oil in a skillet over high heat and sear the beef on all sides until browned, about 2-3 minutes per side. Remove and let cool.

3. Brush the beef with Dijon mustard.

4. In the same skillet, sauté shallots and garlic in a bit of oil until softened. Add the mushrooms and cook until moisture is released and evaporated, about 10 minutes. Add the wine and cook until the mixture is dry. Remove from heat and

let cool.

5. Lay out the prosciutto on plastic wrap, overlap slightly. Spread the mushroom mixture over the prosciutto, then place the beef on top. Roll it up tightly and refrigerate for 15 minutes.

6. Roll out the puff pastry on a floured surface. Unwrap the beef and place it in the center of the pastry. Fold the pastry over the beef, sealing the edges. Brush with egg wash.

7. Bake for 25-30 minutes, or until the pastry is golden brown and the beef reaches your desired doneness. Let rest for 10 minutes before slicing.

Fried Chicken and Mashed Potatoes

Fried Chicken Ingredients:

- 4 chicken pieces (drumsticks, thighs, breasts)
- 1 cup buttermilk
- 1 tbsp hot sauce (optional)
- 1 cup all-purpose flour
- 1 tsp garlic powder
- 1 tsp onion powder
- 1 tsp paprika
- Salt and pepper to taste
- Vegetable oil for frying

Mashed Potatoes Ingredients:

- 4 large russet potatoes, peeled and cut into chunks
- 1/2 cup milk
- 1/4 cup butter
- Salt and pepper to taste

Fried Chicken Instructions:

1. In a bowl, mix the buttermilk and hot sauce. Place the chicken pieces in the mixture and refrigerate for at least 2 hours (or overnight).

2. In a shallow dish, mix flour, garlic powder, onion powder, paprika, salt, and pepper.

3. Heat vegetable oil in a deep skillet or fryer to 350°F (175°C).

4. Dredge each piece of chicken in the flour mixture, coating evenly. Fry the chicken in batches for 10-12 minutes, or until golden brown and the internal temperature reaches 165°F (75°C).

5. Drain on paper towels and serve.

Mashed Potatoes Instructions:

1. Boil the potatoes in salted water until tender, about 15-20 minutes.

2. Drain and return to the pot. Mash with a potato masher or use a hand mixer.

3. Add milk, butter, salt, and pepper. Mix until smooth and creamy.

4. Serve the fried chicken alongside the mashed potatoes.

Ratatouille

Ingredients:

- 1 eggplant, diced
- 1 zucchini, diced
- 1 bell pepper, chopped
- 1 onion, chopped
- 3 tomatoes, chopped
- 2 cloves garlic, minced
- 1/4 cup olive oil
- 1 tsp dried thyme
- 1 tsp dried basil
- Salt and pepper to taste
- Fresh basil for garnish

Instructions:

1. Heat olive oil in a large skillet over medium heat.
2. Add onion and garlic and sauté until softened, about 5 minutes.
3. Add eggplant and bell pepper, cooking for an additional 5 minutes.
4. Add zucchini, tomatoes, thyme, and basil. Season with salt and pepper.
5. Simmer for 20-25 minutes, stirring occasionally, until the vegetables are tender and the flavors have melded together.

6. Garnish with fresh basil before serving.

Beef Chili with Cornbread

Beef Chili Ingredients:

- 1 lb ground beef
- 1 onion, chopped
- 2 cloves garlic, minced
- 1 can (15 oz) diced tomatoes
- 1 can (15 oz) kidney beans, drained
- 1 can (15 oz) black beans, drained
- 1 tbsp chili powder
- 1 tsp cumin
- 1 tsp paprika
- Salt and pepper to taste

Cornbread Ingredients:

- 1 cup cornmeal
- 1 cup all-purpose flour
- 1/4 cup sugar
- 1 tbsp baking powder
- 1/2 tsp salt
- 1 cup milk

- 1/2 cup melted butter

- 2 eggs

Beef Chili Instructions:

1. In a large pot, brown the ground beef over medium heat. Drain excess fat.

2. Add onion and garlic and cook until softened, about 5 minutes.

3. Add diced tomatoes, beans, chili powder, cumin, paprika, salt, and pepper. Stir to combine.

4. Simmer on low heat for 30 minutes, stirring occasionally. Adjust seasoning if needed.

Cornbread Instructions:

1. Preheat the oven to 375°F (190°C).

2. In a large bowl, combine cornmeal, flour, sugar, baking powder, and salt.

3. In a separate bowl, whisk together milk, melted butter, and eggs.

4. Pour the wet ingredients into the dry ingredients and stir until just combined.

5. Pour the batter into a greased 9-inch square baking dish.

6. Bake for 25-30 minutes, or until a toothpick inserted into the center comes out clean.

7. Serve the chili with a side of cornbread.

Shrimp Scampi

Ingredients:

- 1 lb large shrimp, peeled and deveined
- 8 oz linguine or spaghetti
- 3 tbsp olive oil
- 4 cloves garlic, minced
- 1/4 cup white wine
- 1/4 cup chicken broth
- 1/2 tsp red pepper flakes
- 2 tbsp lemon juice
- Salt and pepper to taste
- Fresh parsley, chopped (for garnish)

Instructions:

1. Cook the pasta according to package instructions. Drain and set aside.
2. In a large skillet, heat olive oil over medium-high heat. Add garlic and sauté for 1 minute, until fragrant.
3. Add the shrimp and cook for 2-3 minutes, until pink and cooked through.
4. Add white wine, chicken broth, red pepper flakes, and lemon juice. Simmer for 2-3 minutes to reduce the sauce slightly.
5. Toss the cooked pasta in the skillet with the shrimp and sauce.

6. Garnish with fresh parsley and serve.

Grilled Pork Chops

Ingredients:

- 4 bone-in pork chops
- 2 tbsp olive oil
- 1 tbsp garlic powder
- 1 tbsp onion powder
- 1 tsp smoked paprika
- Salt and pepper to taste

Instructions:

1. Preheat the grill to medium-high heat.
2. Rub the pork chops with olive oil and season with garlic powder, onion powder, smoked paprika, salt, and pepper.
3. Grill the pork chops for 4-5 minutes per side, or until the internal temperature reaches 145°F (63°C).
4. Let the pork chops rest for 5 minutes before serving.

www.ingramcontent.com/pod-product-compliance
Lightning Source LLC
LaVergne TN
LVHW081615060526
838201LV00054B/2264